MW01153641

UNDERSTANDING
BLINDNESS

JESSICA RUSICK

Big Buddy Books

An Imprint of Abdo Publishing
abdobooks.com

abdobooks.com

Published by Abdo Publishing, a division of ABDO, PO Box 398166, Minneapolis, Minnesota 55439.

Printed in the United States of America, North Mankato, Minnesota.
052021
092021

 THIS BOOK CONTAINS RECYCLED MATERIALS

Design: Emily O'Malley, Mighty Media, Inc.
Production: Mighty Media, Inc.
Editor: Megan Borgert-Spaniol
Content Consultant: Brenda Blackmore, Special Education Director
Cover Photographs: Shutterstock Images
Interior Photographs: FatCamera/iStockphoto, pp. 7, 19 (top); huePhotography/iStockphoto, p. 19 (bottom); IvanJekic/iStockphoto, p. 11; Shutterstock Images, pp. 4, 5, 6, 8, 9, 10, 12, 13, 14, 15, 16, 17, 18, 20, 21, 22, 23, 24, 25, 27, 28, 29

Library of Congress Control Number: 2020949911

Publisher's Cataloging-in-Publication Data
Names: Rusick, Jessica, author.
Title: Understanding blindness / by Jessica Rusick
Description: Minneapolis, Minnesota : Abdo Publishing, 2022 | Series: Understanding disabilities | Includes online resources and index.
Identifiers: ISBN 9781532195730 (lib. bdg.) | ISBN 9781098216467 (ebook)
Subjects: LCSH: Blindness--Juvenile literature. | Blind people--Juvenile literature. | People with visual disabilities--Juvenile literature. | Vision disorders--Juvenile literature. | Social acceptance--Juvenile literature.
Classification: DDC 362.41--dc23

CONTENTS

Heading Home

It's the end of another school day for Alex. She uses her cane to make her way through hallways and down steps. Once outside, she walks to the buses. Her bus driver calls out her name. This helps Alex know where her bus is.

Alex is blind. She **experiences** the world differently than sighted people. But she is like any other kid!

What Is Blindness?

Blindness is the condition of having low or no **vision**. Blindness can be **partial** or complete. People who are partially blind have limited vision. But many still **identify** as blind.

It's important to accept and **appreciate** people's differences. You can show you accept and appreciate others by trying to learn about them. You might politely ask whether they'll share with you how being blind affects them.

People with low vision may wear glasses to make what they can see a little clearer.

7

Always use respectful language. Name-calling is never okay. Also, some blind people dislike the term "visually **impaired**." They believe this term suggests they are missing something that they should have.

Remember

People with disabilities are not **victims**. This word makes it sound like having a disability is a bad thing. But a disability is not bad. It's just a difference!

Be sure to respect how a person who is blind chooses to **identify**. It's best to ask which kind of language a person prefers.

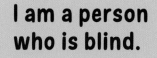

I am a person who is blind.

Person First

Person-first language puts a person before his or her disability. People who use it believe people should not be defined by their disabilities.

I am a blind person.

Identity First

People who use **identity**-first language believe someone's disability is an important part of his or her identity. Some blind people prefer to identify as such.

Who Is Blind?

About 285 million people in the world are blind. Of these, about 39 million people are completely blind. Some people are born blind. Others become blind due to illness or **injury**. A person can become blind for these reasons at any age. In addition, it is common for people to **experience** loss of **vision** as they become older.

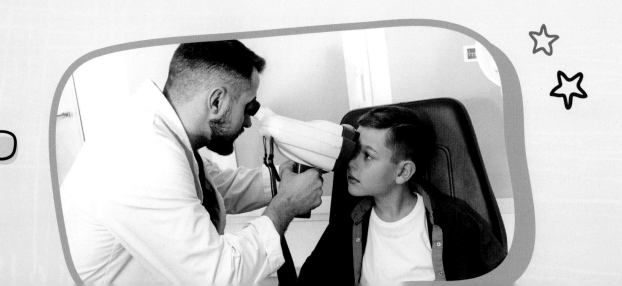

In the United States, 3 percent of children are completely or partially blind.

11

Levels of Blindness

A person who is completely blind does not see anything, including light. However, many blind people can see light. Others have some limited sight of colors and objects.

A person does not need to be completely blind to be considered **legally** blind. A legally blind person can see an object from 20 feet (6 m) away when a sighted person can see it from 200 feet (61 m) away.

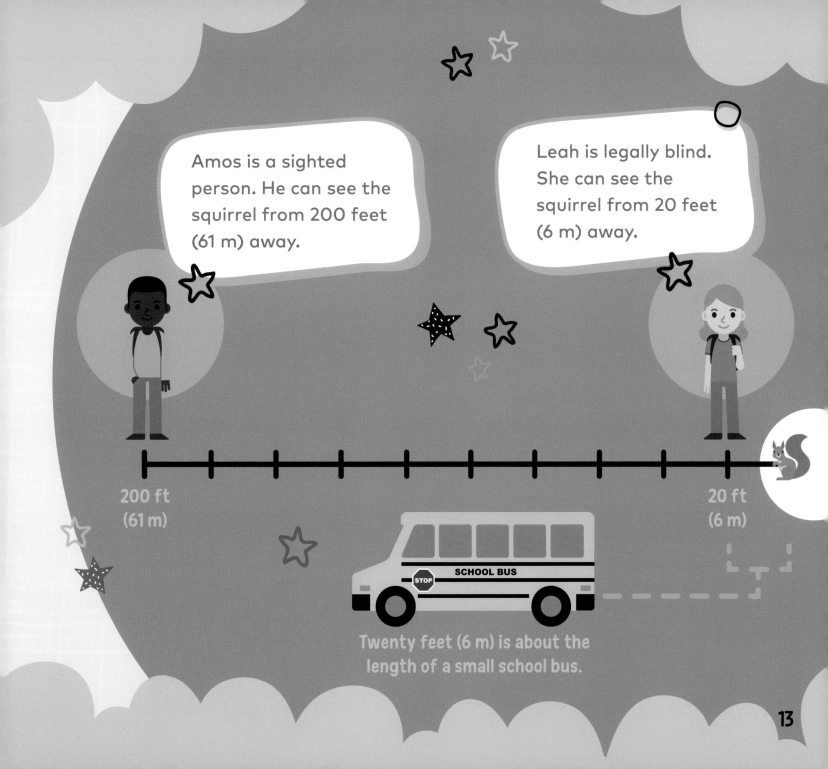

Amos is a sighted person. He can see the squirrel from 200 feet (61 m) away.

Leah is legally blind. She can see the squirrel from 20 feet (6 m) away.

200 ft (61 m)

20 ft (6 m)

Twenty feet (6 m) is about the length of a small school bus.

Getting Around

People who are blind use several skills and **mobility** aids to get around.

Memory

In familiar places, blind people often depend on memory to move around.

Senses

Blind people often use hearing, touch, and even smell to safely move from place to place.

Canes

Some blind people sweep or tap canes side to side while walking. Canes allow blind people to sense sidewalks, curbs, and **obstacles**.

Guide Dogs

Guide dogs are trained **service animals**. They help blind people avoid obstacles when walking. They can also help find the entrances to buildings.

Helping Hands

A sighted person can help guide a blind person from place to place.

Reading

Many blind kids read using braille. This is a system of raised dots that stand for letters, numbers, and words. People read braille by moving their fingers over the dots.

Braille allows blind people to read books, music, signs, and more. Kids with limited **vision** may also read large-print books. These are books in which the words are bigger and easier to see.

Braille sign

Braille uses groups of up to six raised dots. To read braille, kids must remember many different dot arrangements.

Blindness at School

Some blind children learn at schools for blind students. Other blind kids learn in sighted classrooms. Different **devices** and practices help blind students succeed.

Braille Displays

Braille displays are devices that connect to computers. The display turns words on the computer screen into braille dots.

Screen Reading

Screen reading **software** helps blind kids use computers. These programs turn words and pictures on a computer screen into spoken words.

Classroom Aide

A classroom aide is a person who helps guide and **describe** things to a blind student. An aide can also help change written schoolwork into braille.

Social Challenges

Some blind kids face social **challenges**. Sighted people learn many social skills by watching other people. This includes how close to stand to someone when talking. It may sometimes take longer for blind kids to learn these skills.

Blind kids may also be teased for appearing different. Being teased makes people feel bad about themselves.

21

Being a Friend

Everyone has his or her own strengths and **challenges**. That's okay! No matter what, everyone should be treated with respect.

There are many ways to be a good friend to someone who is blind. Let a blind friend know when you are approaching or leaving. It is also okay to offer your friend help. But make sure to respect her answer. Sometimes she may welcome help. Other times, she may not need it.

A blind friend may ask to hold your arm while crossing a street. But don't assume she needs help.

More Ways to Be a Friend

Speak Normally

You don't have to speak any differently to a blind friend. There is no need to raise your voice.

Stand Up to Bullying

Let an adult know if your friend is being teased.

Guide Dogs

Don't pet a friend's guide dog without permission. The guide dog is doing an important job and shouldn't be **distracted**.

Strengths

Being blind can be **challenging**. However, many people find their blindness makes them good at listening and **multitasking**. This is because they often pay close attention to several sounds at a time. Blind people have become successful writers, singers, sports stars, and more.

Molly Burke

Molly Burke is a blind YouTube star. She was bullied in school. This **experience** made her want to help others. Burke shares her story to educate people and bring hope to those who need it.

Molly Burke at the 2017 YouTube Streamy Awards with her guide dog, Gallop

Golden Rules

Millions of people have disabilities. If you know someone with a disability, there may be times when you feel unsure of what to say or do. When in doubt, remember to treat others how you'd want to be treated. And, keep in mind these other golden rules:

* Accept and respect differences
* Use respectful language
* Be kind and caring

Activities

Do you have any friends who are blind? Invite them to join you for a fun activity.

Listen to music together

Go for a nature walk

Play Jenga or a similar stacking game

GLOSSARY

appreciate—to value or admire greatly.

challenge (CHA-luhnj)—something that tests one's strengths or abilities.

describe—to tell about something with words.

device—an object or machine that has a certain job.

distract—to cause to turn away from one's original focus.

experience—to do, see, feel, or be affected by something. Something that happens to you is an experience.

identify—to say or show who someone is.

identity—the set of features and beliefs that make a person who she or he is.

impair—to make less or worse.

injury (IHN-juh-ree)—hurt or loss received.

legal—based on or allowed by law.

mobility—the ability to move or be moved.

multitask—to do more than one activity at the same time.

obstacle—something that you have to go over or around.

partial—not complete.

service animal—an animal trained to do tasks for someone with a disability.

software—a program or programs that run on a computer.

victim—someone who has been harmed by an unpleasant event.

vision—the ability to see.

ONLINE RESOURCES

Booklinks
NONFICTION NETWORK
FREE! ONLINE NONFICTION RESOURCES

To learn more about blindness, please visit **abdobooklinks.com** or scan this QR code. These links are routinely monitored and updated to provide the most current information available.

INDEX